MARIE M. CLAY

CONCEPTS ABOUT PRINT

What have children learned about the way we print language?

Heinemann

KH

Published by Heinemann Education, a division of Reed Publishing (NZ) Ltd, 39 Rawene Road, Birkenhead, Auckland, New Zealand. Associated companies, branches and representatives throughout the world.

In the United States: Heinemann, a division of Reed Publishing (USA) Inc. 361 Hanover Street, Portsmouth, NH 03801-3912.

ISBN 0 86863 298 8 (NZ)

Library of Congress Cataloging-in-Publication Data
CIP data is on file with the Library of Congress.
ISBN 0 325 00237 1 (USA)

© 2000, Marie M. Clay

Printed in Singapore

The pronouns she and he have often been used in this text to refer to the teacher and the child respectively. Despite a possible charge of sexist bias it makes for clearer, easier reading if such references are consistent.

The author and publishers permit the following observation record sheets to be copied by teachers for use with children. The commercial use of any of these observation record sheets is strictly prohibited.

- Concepts About Print Score Sheet – *Follow Me, Moon/No Shoes* page 14
- Concepts About Print Score Sheet – *Sand/Stones* page 30

8/21/05

Contents

1 Observing What Children Have Learned About the Way We Print Language   4

    Concepts About Print are learned gradually   4

    Revealing what children know   5

    How much do children need to know about print?   6

    Reading to the children   6

    Observing progress   7

2 Using the Concepts About Print Observation Task   8

    Administration   8

    Scoring   9

    Interpretation of scores   10

    Administration Instructions – *Follow Me, Moon/No Shoes*   12

    Concepts About Print Score Sheet   *Follow Me, Moon/No Shoes*   14

    Quick Reference for Scoring Standards – *Follow Me, Moon/No Shoes*   15

3 More Technical Background Information on the Concepts About Print Task   16

    1   What does the Concepts About Print task assess?   16

    2   Where did this assessment come from?   17

    3   When is it important to give this task to literacy learners?   18

    4   What do we know from research studies?   20

    5   How might teachers of new entrants use this information?   24

Appendices   27

    APPENDIX 1 – Administration Instructions – *Sand/Stones*   28

    APPENDIX 2 – Concepts About Print Score Sheet – *Sand/Stones*   30

    APPENDIX 3 – Quick Reference for Scoring Standards – *Sand/Stones*   31

References   32

Observing What Children Have Learned About the Way We Print Language

When young children who are just becoming familiar with books are handed a book, what do they do with it? Do they turn the book the right way up? Start at the front? Look for the first page of text? Attend to the picture or to the print? Turn pages in sequence one at a time? Early in literacy learning children must discover something about the arbitrary conventions we have for putting the language we speak into a printed form. How do we print the messages we want others to read? Where does the story begin?

This is sometimes described as 'print awareness'. But that can mean many things. What is learned in a child's first contacts with print are some directional rules for moving through print, and some simple ideas or concepts about how print works.

A colleague recently passed me a children's book written in Hebrew. Without hesitation I turned the book over to look at what would be the back cover of a book written in English but is the front of a Hebrew book. 'Oh!' said my colleague, 'you know something about Hebrew.' In fact I know nothing about Hebrew except the conventions used for writing the language down, but I knew those so well that, without a thought, I immediately went to the starting point. I used some directional concepts that were different from the ones I use when I read English.

Concepts About Print are learned gradually

As children engage with printed messages and books they learn some things about looking through a story in sequence. However, there is still a great deal more to learn about the writing code, and it is learned gradually over an extended period of time. There is no way to explain 'a code' simply, so it is better not to try to explain it in words for that would confuse most young children. A good diet of book-sharing in the preschool years, plus warm responses to their efforts to find things in print or make messages by writing print, will help children when they go off to school. At that time they will know a few things about print.

As a result of their preschool opportunities different children will know different things. It is not really a question of how much they know; it is more a matter of what they do know and what they have yet to sort out about language in print.

Where does one start? In what direction does one move? How does one move through a word? These are features of any written message, especially when it is longer than a word. If we are only thinking of single letters or words it is not too difficult but a couple of lines of print can be very confusing! Parents and teachers who see some children fall easily into appropriate ways of looking at print often underestimate how extraordinarily complex it is to understand some of the rules of the written code, and how easy it is to pick up strange ways, which can become habits, of attending to a page of print.

Revealing what children know

Teachers can use the Concepts About Print (C.A.P.) story booklets to discover some of the things children already know about print, and what has yet to be learned. This is a task which allows teachers, quite reliably, to see who needs what kind of help. It shows a teacher which of the children need more teacher attention. Intensive opportunities to learn what many other children at school entry already know may be needed at school entry, and at other times during the first two years at school. The group requiring extra help may be quite large in some schools. Research with children of different cultural groups in New Zealand, over several decades, has shown that what is known about letters, sounds and words begins to expand rapidly once the learner has an understanding of some of these concepts. *The teacher's goal is to help the learner to get beyond having to give close attention to 'the rules of the road'.*

How much do children need to know about print?

Eventually children need to follow all the rules but this learning will come mostly from the opportunities they have to read and write at school. It is a good idea to discover what children already know about books and print because there can be large individual differences in what they can attend to. The differences are not just in how much they know, but also in the fact that one child will understand some aspects of reading and writing which are quite different from the things another child has learned to pay attention to. Teachers must become *interested* in the differences.

It is easy to observe what children already know by using this observation task, and a teacher will be better prepared to advance any child's understanding when she or he already knows what children are attending to. *That is what Concepts About Print is designed to reveal – what children are attending to, rightly or wrongly.*

Of course the understanding of some of these arbitrary rules for setting down language in a written form (in short, these concepts about print) is only one aspect of literacy learning: other aspects of literacy learning can be observed with different observation tasks. *An Observation Survey of Early Literacy Achievement* (Clay, 1993) recommends that teachers observe several different aspects of children's literacy learning. The learner needs more than one key to unlock the code. When a child understands what to attend to, in what order, and a few things about the shapes and positions of letters and words, this opens other doors to literacy learning.

Reading to the children

In the Concepts About Print observation task the teacher appears to be merely reading the story in the test booklet to the child but she is also asking the child to help. On each page she asks a question or two. She finds out what the child knows about print: the front of a book, that print (not the picture) tells the story, that there are letters, and clusters of letters called words, that there are first letters and last letters in words, that you can choose upper

Teachers can choose one of four alternate Concepts About Print stories.

and lower case letters, that spaces are there for a reason, and that different punctuation marks signal meanings (full stop or period, question mark, speech marks).

Even when we give such things a name or try to explain some of these things to children we cannot assume that our verbal explanations have taught children to use their eyes to locate, recognise or otherwise make use of such information. These concepts are learned gradually in reading and writing activities over the first two years of formal schooling.

Special booklets have been prepared for this observation task, entitled *Sand* (1972), *Stones* (1979), *Follow Me, Moon* (2000) and *No Shoes* (2000). They can be used with non-readers or beginning readers; before beginning school or after a time in instruction. The child is asked to help the observer by pointing to certain features of the text while the book is being read. Five-year-old children have some fun and little difficulty with the tasks.

Observing progress

The observation task should be given in a standard way because then it can reflect changes in reading competency during the first and second year of school. Children do not need to be able to talk about these concepts. If they can work with them and pay them very little attention they have what is needed to underpin subsequent progress. For problem readers confusions with these arbitrary conventions of a written language code can persist and interfere with effective learning.

The Concepts About Print tasks have proved to be sensitive indicators of one group of behaviours which supports reading and writing acquisition, but the test score cannot be expected to stand alone as a prediction device or an indicator of readiness. The concepts are things the child *must* come to understand. Becoming involved with literacy activities will help them to grasp some, and eventually all, of these necessary concepts. Sooner is better than later. It would be absurd to try to build learning activities to teach such concepts before a child is engaged in some kind of reading and writing experiences. These things go hand in hand.

Important discussions about these concepts are to be found in titles in the reference list (page 32).

2 Using the Concepts About Print Observation Task

Administration

Before starting, thoroughly familiarise yourself with the Concepts About Print story that you intend to use, the record sheet and the administration instructions. Giving this assessment in a valid way requires prior practice. Despite the questions which ask for the child's help, the story must be read with sufficient continuity and vitality for the child to be able to gain its meaning and a sense of the flow. Avoid adding extra comments.

Develop a standard way of using this observation task, *always reading from the administration guide*, following the instructions with precision, and making sure that the child understands what he or she is being asked to do. Position the sheet with the instructions in this teacher's guide to the side away from the child. After the first item has been given, the book (*Follow Me, Moon, No Shoes, Sand* or *Stones*) should be placed between you and the child so that you can both see it easily. To keep the scoring unobtrusive, you may want to mark incomplete or incorrect responses with a dot, and fill in markings and scores for correct responses after the assessment session is over.

To make administration easier, plan your seating and layout arrangements before you begin.

Administer the items as directed. The instructions for giving and scoring this test are given on pages 12-13. You will need a copy of the scoring sheet on page 14 for every child. The guide for scoring each item on page 15 can be consulted later.

Read the instructions to the child, as they are written, for each item. Use the *exact* wording given in each demonstration. Move deliberately and demonstrate clearly.

If the child does not respond appropriately to Item 10, then items 12, 13 and 14 are likely to be difficult and *can be omitted at the discretion of the observer*. You should still read the story on those pages to the child. Items 15 to 24 should then be administered to all children. (On items 10, 12, 13 and 14 your position and movement can ensure that the child is attending to the print.)

Scoring

Mark the child's responses as instructed. You can simply total the number of items passed, and note what the child knows and what has yet to be learned.

Alternatively by using one of the tables on page 10 you can read off a scale of scores from 1 to 9.* This scaled score provides a guide to how well the child compares with a sample of children of the 5-7 age group. Choose the first table if you are assessing five-year-old children, or if the average stanine of 5 seems to fit with average progress in your school. Choose the second table if you are assessing six-year-old children or if your children move quickly in this area. Choose the Ohio stanines if you prefer a comparison sample from the United States. Read the later section on interpretation if you have difficulty selecting a table.

It is possible for an education system to build up its own table of stanine scores. In any school teachers could accumulate data over several years against which to compare each child, or each year's intake of children on this aspect of literacy learning.

---

* These are called stanine scores and they distribute the scores of the research sample according to a normal curve into nine groups (see *An Observation Survey of Early Literacy Achievement* for more detailed information on stanines, reliability and validity).

Concepts About Print (Normalised Scores)

320 New Zealand urban children aged 5 : 0 - 7 : 0 in 1968	Stanine group	1	2	3	4	5	6	7	8	9
	Test score	0	1–4	5–7	8–11	12–14	15–17	18–20	21–22	23–24

282 New Zealand urban children aged 6 : 0 - 7 : 3 in 1978	Stanine group	1	2	3	4	5	6	7	8	9
	Test score	0–9	10–11	12–13	14–16	17–18	19	20–21	22	23–24

73 Ohio urban children in first grade in 1990-91	Stanine group	1	2	3	4	5	6	7	8	9
	Test score	0–10	11–12	13	14–15	16	17–18	19	20	21–24

The main purpose of the scale is to provide teachers with a reference number or group for a child's score at initial testing so that changes in that child's performance can be recorded six, 12 or 18 months later. To be a successful reader a child must come to control all the concepts tested by this task. Change occurs from (a) having a little knowledge, towards (b) having a control of all these concepts within about two years of beginning literacy learning.

Interpretation of scores

The concepts about print measured in this observation task are a limited set of information which can be learned in the first years of school. The task's greatest value is the guidance that it gives to teachers. Items uncover concepts yet to be learned or confusions to be untangled. Young children get low scores early in their schooling, and their scores should increase as their reading and writing improves. Teachers should see a control over these concepts gradually emerging, and retests at spaced intervals will show that change is occurring.

For teaching purposes examine the child's performance and then gradually teach the unknown concepts. *The items are not in a difficulty sequence* because the reading of the story did not allow for this. Some indication of difficulty level for New Zealand children is given in the Age Expectations Table (page 11) which gives the age at which average children passed each item. Notice which items children find difficult at first and tend to learn later. What is easy or difficult will be highly dependent on the teaching programme and method or emphases used in any particular school.

Most of these Concepts About Print items tell us something about what the children are attending to on the printed page. In items 12 to 14, (1) the order of words, or (2) letters at the beginning or end of words, or (3) letters in the middle of words, have been changed. These items are particularly sensitive to shifts in what children are attending to as they look at print. There is *a very steep gradient of difficulty on items 12 to 14*. Children usually notice the changed word order (Item 12) before a change in first and last letters (Item 13) or a change in the letters buried within the word (Item 14). And many children take a long time to sort out the difference between what people call a word and what people call a letter!

Concepts that a child had difficulty with can be developed within a balanced literacy programme, where the child and teacher explore a variety of texts and focus on particular needs that have been identified (Learning Media, 1997).

AGE EXPECTATIONS FOR ITEMS																								
(Age at which 50 percent of average European children pass an item; Clay, 1970)																								
ITEM	1	2	3	4	5	6	7	8	9	10	11	12	13	14	15	16	17	18	19	20	21	22	23	24
Age 5:0		x																						
5:6	x		x	x	x	x	x	x	x	x	x										x			
6:0																			x	x		x		
6:6												x	x		x								x	x
7:0														x		x	x	x						

Say to the child: '*I'm going to read you this story but I want you to help me.*'

COVER

Item 1   Test: For orientation of book. Pass the book to the child, holding it vertically by outside edge, spine towards the child.

Say: '*Show me the front of this book.*'

Score: 1 point for the correct response.

PAGES 2/3

Item 2   Test: Concept that print, not picture, carries the message.

Say: '*I'll read this story. You help me. Show me where to start reading. Where do I begin to read?*'

Read the text on page 2.

Score: 1 point for print. 0 for picture.

PAGES 4/5

Item 3   Test: For directional rules.

Say: '*Show me where to start.*'

Score: 1 point for top left.

Item 4   Test: Moves left to right on any line.

Say: '*Which way do I go?*'

Score: 1 point for left to right.

Item 5   Test: Return sweep.

Say: '*Where do I go after that?*'

Score: 1 point for return sweep to left, or for moving down the page.

(Score items 3-5 if all movements are demonstrated in one response.)

Item 6   Test: Word-by-word pointing.

Say: '*Point to it while I read it.*'

Read the text on page 4 slowly but fluently.

Score: 1 point for exact matching.

PAGE 6

Item 7   Test: Concept of first and last.

Read the text on page 6.

Say: '*Show me the first part of the story.*'
'*Show me the last part.*'

Score: 1 point if BOTH are correct in any sense, that is, applied to the whole text or to a line, or to a word, or to a letter.

PAGE 7

Item 8   Test: Inversion of picture.

Say: (slowly and deliberately) '*Show me the bottom of the picture.*'
(DO NOT MENTION UPSIDE-DOWN.)

Score: 1 point for verbal explanation, OR for pointing to top of page, OR for turning the book around and pointing appropriately.

PAGES 8/9

Item 9   Test: Response to inverted print.

Say: '*Where do I begin?*'
'*Which way do I go?*'
'*Where do I go after that?*'

Score: 1 point for beginning with 'I' (*Moon*), or 'Leaves' (*Shoes*), and moving right to left across the lower and then the upper line. OR 1 point for turning the book around and moving left to right in the conventional manner.

Read the text on page 8 now.

PAGES 10/11

Item 10   Test: Line sequence.

Say: '*What's wrong with this?*'

Read immediately the bottom line first, then the top line. Do NOT point.

Score: 1 point for comment on line order.

PAGES 12/13

Item 11   Test: A left page is read before a right page.

Say: '*Where do I start reading?*'

Score: 1 point for indicating the left page.

Item 12   Test: Word sequence.

Say: '*What's wrong on this page?*' (Point to **page number 12**, NOT the text.)

Read the text on page 12 slowly as if it were correctly printed.

Score: 1 point for comment on either error.

Item 13   Test: Letter order. (Changes to first or last letters.)

Say: '*What's wrong on this page?*' (Point to **page number 13**, NOT the text.)

Read the text on page 13 slowly as if it were correctly printed.

Score: 1 point for any ONE re-ordering of letters that is noticed and explained.

Item 14   Test: Re-ordering of letters within a word.

           Say: *'What's wrong with the writing on this page?'*

Read the text on page 14 slowly as if it were correctly printed.

           Score: 1 point for ONE error noticed.

Item 15   Test: Meaning of a question mark.

           Say: *'What's this for?'* (Point to or trace the question mark with a finger or pencil.)

           Score: 1 point for explanation of function or name.

           Test: Punctuation.

Read the text on page 16.

           Say: *'What's this for?'*

Item 16   Point to or trace with a pencil, the full stop (period).

Item 17   Point to or trace with a pencil, the comma.

Item 18   Point to or trace with a pencil, the quotation marks.

Item 19   Test: Capital and lower case letters.

           Say: *'Find a little letter like this.'*

           Moon: Point to capital P and demonstrate by pointing to an upper case P and a lower case p if the child does not succeed.

           Shoes: As above for W and w.

           Say: *'Find a little letter like this.'*

           Moon: Point to capital M, I in turn.

           Shoes: Point to capital M, I in turn.

           Score: *Moon*: 1 point if BOTH m and i are located.

                      Shoes: 1 point if BOTH m and i are located.

Item 20   Test: Words that contain the same letters in a different order.

Read the text on page 18.

           Say: *'Show me* was.*'*
                   'Show me no.*'*

            Score: 1 point for BOTH correct.

Have two pieces of light card (13 cm x 5 cm) that the child can hold and slide easily over the line of text to block out words and letters. To start, lay the cards on the page but leave all print exposed. Open the cards out between each question asked.

Item 21   Test: Letter concepts.

           Say: *'This story says (**Moon**) "The moon followed me home" [or (**Shoes**) "My shoes were by the river"]. I want you to push the cards across the story like this until all you can see is* (deliberately with stress) *just one letter.'* (Demonstrate the movement of the cards but do not do the exercise.)

           Say: *'Now show me two letters.'*

           Score: 1 point if BOTH are correct.

Item 22   Test: Word concept.

           Say: *'Show me just one word.'*
                   'Now show me two words.'

            Score: 1 point if BOTH are correct.

Item 23   Test: First and last letter concepts.

           Say: *'Show me the first letter of a word.'*
                   'Show me the last letter of a word.'

            Score: 1 point if BOTH are correct.

Item 24   Test: Capital letter concepts.

           Say: *'Show me a capital letter.'*

            Score: 1 point if correct.

CONCEPTS ABOUT PRINT SCORE SHEET

Date: _____

Name: _____ Age: _____ TEST SCORE: [/24]

Recorder: _____ Date of Birth: _____ STANINE GROUP: [   ]

PAGE	SCORE	ITEM	COMMENT
Cover		1. Front of book	
2/3		2. Print contains message	
4/5		3. Where to start	
4/5		4. Which way to go	
4/5		5. Return sweep to left	
4/5		6. Word-by-word matching	
6		7. First and last concept	
7		8. Bottom of picture	
8/9		9. Begins 'I' (*Moon*) or 'Leaves' (*Shoes*) bottom line, top OR turns book	
10/11		10. Line order altered	
12/13		11. Left page before right	
12/13		12. One change in word order	
12/13		13. One change in letter order	
14/15		14. One change in letter order	
14/15		15. Meaning of a question mark	
16/17		16. Meaning of full stop (period)	
16/17		17. Meaning of comma	
16/17		18. Meaning of quotation marks	
16/17		19. Locate m i (*Moon*) OR m i (*Shoes*)	
18/19		20. Reversible words *was, no*	
20		21. One letter: two letters	
20		22. One word: two words	
20		23. First and last letter of word	
20		24. Capital letter	

QUICK REFERENCE FOR SCORING STANDARDS

Item	Pass standard
1	Front of book.
2	Print (not picture).
3	Points top left at 'I said …' (*Moon*) or 'When I …' (*Shoes*).
4	Moves finger left to right on any line.
5	Moves finger from the right-hand end of a higher line to the left-hand end of the next lower line, or moves down the page.
6	Word-by-word matching.
7	Both concepts must be correct, but may be demonstrated on the whole text or on a line, word or letter.
8	Verbal explanation, or pointing to top of page, or turning the book around and pointing appropriately.
9	Score for beginning with 'I ran' (*Moon*) or 'Leaves' (*Shoes*) and moving right to left across the lower line and then the upper line, OR turning the book around and moving left to right in the conventional movement pattern.
10	Any explanation which implies that line order is altered.
11	Says or shows that a left page precedes a right page.
12	Notices at least one change of word order.
13	Notices at least one change in letter order.
14	Notices at least one change in letter order.
15	Says 'Question mark', or 'A question', or 'Asks something'.
16	Says 'Full stop', 'Period', 'It tells you when you've said enough' or 'It's the end'.
17	Says 'A little stop', or 'A rest', or 'A comma'.
18	Says 'That's someone talking', 'Talking', 'Speech marks'.
19	Locates two capital and lower case pairs.
20	Points correctly to **both** *was* and *no*.
21	Locates one letter and two letters on request.
22	Locates one word and two words on request.
23	Locates both a first and a last letter.
24	Locates one capital letter.

Clay, 1993, page 51

3 More Technical Background Information on the Concepts About Print Task

The Concepts About Print (C.A.P.) task is a specialised task, designed to help teachers observe young children's growing recognition of the conventions and characteristics of a written language (Harris and Hodges, 1995). It can be used at any time between five and seven years, and sometimes outside those age limits. Five questions provide a useful framework for reviewing how this task has been reported in the academic literature:

1 What does the Concepts About Print (C.A.P.) task assess?
2 Where did this assessment come from?
3 When is it important to give this task to literacy learners?
4 What do we know from research studies?
5 How might new entrant teachers use this information?

1 What does the Concepts About Print task assess?

In simplest terms it reveals what the learner is attending to, both appropriately and inappropriately. To support learning a teacher needs to know what the learner is attending to. In the daily activities of the classroom, teachers can be good observers of what children know about literacy, and they find it relatively easy to see and hear what children know about letters and sounds, or about words. However, the knowledge tapped by C.A.P. requires a well-designed task to uncover what children are attending to. It informs teachers about the literacy learning that already exists.

The concepts that children need to learn about print include directional movement, one-to-one matching of spoken words to printed words, and book conventions. Skilful teaching is required to focus the students' attention on the details of print while ensuring that the message of the text and the enjoyment of the story are not lost (Learning Media, 1996).

2   Where did this assessment come from?

In a research project I described what a sample of five-year-old children did as they tried to read simple introductory reading books (Clay, 1982). I wrote down everything they said and everything they did. After thinking a great deal about what I saw in my research records, I took three little books published in England, identical in layout and sentence structure but different in content, and devised some tasks that children of this age might do with such a book. I even undid the staples and turned pictures and text upside down. The new tasks looked promising for showing teachers what I had been able to observe about children's responding.

As an educational psychologist I could draw on my experience of testing preschool and school-age children, of knowing how to engage their attention, and what makes for good and bad items in tests to be used with this young age group. I began to refine my pilot tasks. I was trying to capture the awareness of print observed in children before they had been taught to read, so the task could not involve asking the children to read, write or name any feature of print. When I read a simple story to them the assessment task involved asking the child to act in some way, such as turning a page or pointing to something on request, so that children could show, rather than have to tell, what they knew.

Trials and test development procedures led to an observation survey of several literacy tasks (Clay, 1972, 1993), with C.A.P. as one of six parts. This survey could be used by classroom teachers for the systematic observation of young children's progress at any time during the first two years of school. Progress is the key word because the survey is designed to capture what change is occurring during this period. In New Zealand the survey is usually given after one year at school. One challenge has been to convince teachers to be systematic about identifying children who are making much slower progress with literacy learning than their classmates. Teachers perform a balancing act of allowing children time to engage with the school's programme but avoiding having them drop too far behind their faster learning classmates before a systematic assessment is made. My longitudinal research (Clay, 1967) showed how, under the careful tutelage of their teachers, individual children became readers and writers in their first year of school. However, some were taking a long time to get started and were falling further and further behind their faster classmates.

So, the Concepts About Print task, designed at first to observe the early progress of five-year-old school entrants in a research study, became part of a survey which could quantify the progress of high, middle and low progress children after one year at school. Much later, in 1978, this survey was also used to select children for Reading Recovery, a specific programme for children who need more assistance in literacy learning than they can get in their classrooms, and who receive a period of individual instruction to boost their progress. So, the survey is a way to observe (1) all beginners, (2) progress in the next two years, and (3) children selected for special help. Concepts About Print reveals one kind of learning essential to early progress in literacy learning.

3 When is it important to give this task to literacy learners?

When young children who are just becoming familiar with books are handed a book, what do they attend to? One of the first codebreaking activities in reading is to discover something about the arbitrary conventions of how printed messages are presented. I demonstrated this to my undergraduate classes by distributing children's storybooks from Japan and Israel and letting them observe their own confusions with a different approach to book organisation from the one they were used to for English.

Recent research has opened our eyes to how much preschool children notice about 'language in print' before they come to school. The flip side of that understanding is that we also know that some children have had little opportunity for such learning. Or perhaps they have just taken little notice of print in their environment. This happens even when they are moving around in a print-saturated environment. Some adults believe that literacy is 'school territory' and best left until children start school so they do not try to foster literacy learning, whereas other adults advocate providing rich literacy learning opportunities in the preschool years. Children are vastly different in the attention they give to print. Teachers know this, and they also know that those who are more aware of print move into reading and writing ahead of those who do not. Children bring different amounts of prior knowledge to the new challenges that the school provides.

Child development theories have taught us that healthy children with many learning opportunities, sound emotional development, good motor control and good language will tend to be successful in school. And research in the last two decades has convinced most educators that what preschoolers learn about books and written messages can make school literacy learning a little easier. Over the first few months of school teachers need to observe specific literacy behaviours as well as the more general indicators of individual differences.

There is a particular reason why learners need to grasp book and print orientation skills early. The conventions of written language control how readers direct their attention, that is, what they attend to, and in which order. The order of letters and words is of vital importance when children are trying to read and write. Like the traffic conventions which vary from country to country, the conventions of print vary from one writing system to another, but invariably they direct the order in which the reader attends to the print. A wonderful knowledge of letter shapes, or letter sounds, or words cannot serve a reader well if that reader is travelling the wrong way down a one-way street! And, in the beginning, learners survey print in uncontrolled ways, just as we adults survey pictures according to our own preferences. Learning about the arbitrary ways in which we write down what we say is necessary in every language, it seems. Researchers in Germany, Denmark and Israel have now reported on how concepts about print are learned in other languages (Clay, 1989).

Once children have some idea about how books are presented and can look through a story in sequence, there is still a lot more to learn. In what order does one attend to the detail in print? How does one move through a word? Where does one start? In what direction does one move? These things seem unimportant when we think of 'reading' single letters or words but they are features of any message written in continuous text.

Parents and teachers who see some children learn ways of surveying print with little effort, often fail to notice the other children who are becoming very confused, taking a very long time to 'get it all together', or even ignoring these things (see David in Clay, 1991, page 118). C.A.P. can reliably separate children who have such learning under control from those who do not, either at school entry or throughout the first two years of school. It uncovers those who need more teacher attention and intensive make-up opportunities if they are to learn what many preschoolers have already mastered, and the group requiring extra help may, in some schools, include up to half an intake class.

4   What do we know from research studies?

Studies of different language and cultural groups in New Zealand over several decades (McNaughton, 1995) have shown that what is known about letters, sounds and words begins to expand rapidly once these concepts about print no longer need the learner's attention. That is the teaching goal – to do away with the need to give close attention to 'the rules of the road'. Extensive evidence has helped us to understand how, and how fast, children's knowledge about the written code changes throughout their first year at school, once they meet up with expectations that they will learn to read and write.

In my original research the C.A.P. scores of the 100 children studied weekly increased over the first year of school (Clay, 1967, 1982). The performance of both the high-progress and the low-progress groups changed significantly during that year showing that teachers were reaching both groups at their own levels which was good, but members of the low-progress group were about nine months behind the high-progress group. That study provided evidence that responding successfully to the left-to-right rule in written English was not dependent on hand preference or verbal concepts of left and right. A mere feel for the movement in the correct direction that must occur was all that was required; no more than a feeling for a consistent way of approaching certain experiences. Yet a few children became confused about this, and confusion persisted for months.

Directional learning is more likely to be related to learning than maturing. This was supported by a research study of identical quadruplets which showed how individual differences can be created even when genetic and environmental histories are close to identical. It took four same-age sisters, from the same home, kindergarten and first school class, different amounts of time for their directional movements across a text to settle down to a consistent sequence of attention to a text. The time ranged across 12, 26, 38 and 46 weeks respectively, or from three to twelve months at school! Other evidence in this study showed that all four children were teachable once teachers noticed what specifically each child needed to learn (Clay, 1974).

From 1967 to 1991 many studies of early literacy progress in New Zealand classrooms contributed similar evidence although they used different research theories and methods. Space allows for only two to be reviewed here. A detailed observation study based on 15-second intervals was made of eight children in new entrant rooms in 10 Auckland primary schools, that is 80 of the newest of new entrants (Watson, 1980). From many mornings in classrooms tallies showed that 53 percent of teacher moves were related to reading instruction, 20 percent were related to writing instruction, and only 27 percent were not to do with learning to read and write. Whatever the timetable activity the teacher understood that these children were beginners in literacy learning and took opportunities to get the children to attend to printed messages in appropriate ways.

Another study of instruction in the first term of school (Clay, 1985) showed how quickly children came to grips with this foundation for early reading and writing. Teachers brought about progress with very few controlling-type moves and kept their children on task more than 90 percent of the time. They were adept at finding time for individual teaching and they distributed their attention positively and equally across all subgroups studied (European, Maori and Pacific Island groups). Results showed that C.A.P. scores distinguished between those children who knew a great deal about printed language on entry to school at five years and those who knew very little. The scores provided a baseline for all children against which subsequent progress could be judged. In each school new entrants on the average shifted from low C.A.P. on entry to school to knowing half the items tested after only one term at school. This was a time of rapid change for most children (in the European, Maori and Pacific Island groups) and any remaining low scorers were clearly in need of extra time, extra attention and extra ingenuity if they were not to be left behind.

C.A.P. caught the attention of British and American researchers. In 1967 Helen Robinson at the University of Chicago espoused a renewed emphasis on the observation of children's behaviours in the United States. She used one item from C.A.P. as an example. It showed that many beginning readers do not know the boundaries of printed words. This, Robinson reported, led to experimental research by others confirming the results and extending them to spoken words, letters and sounds. She cautioned that the fact that a C.A.P. score might predict progress well would not be as important as its implications for teaching. She emphasised that children need to learn the direction of English print, that children have to learn what a letter is and what a word is, that this is uncertain knowledge at the end of one year at school; that finger-pointing to words and a staccato pronunciation may be an important stage in matching printed words to spoken words; and that the pupil must be given time to respond and must not be harassed if he or she searches at length or if he or she fails to respond.

The *Reading Research Quarterly* published an independent evaluation of C.A.P. (Johns, 1980). Other researchers had shown it to be a reliable and valid test for American children before Jerry Johns studied how it worked with 60 first-grade (six-year-old) children who were above-average, average and below-average readers. He grouped the items according to four patterns under the headings book orientation, print direction, letter-word concepts, and advanced print concepts. All his Grade 1 children obtained perfect scores on book orientation after their year in kindergarten (in the United States), but his above-average readers were superior to below-average readers in the last three categories. His important conclusion was that awareness of concepts about print may exist as both a consequence of what has occurred in a child's life so far and as a cause affecting subsequent school progress. Readers may wonder why this is even questioned because it seems so obvious. However, in the academic hunt for the causes of literacy difficulties which might explain reading progress, the concept of reciprocity (which means that one competency helps and extends a different competency and vice versa) is very hard to control and has only recently appeared in theoretical discussions.

Research which follows children over time shows that learning about book orientation and print direction begins early, but mastery (in the sense that no slips occur) takes a considerable time. The situation is very different for the concepts of a letter and a word. Below-average readers confuse the concepts of a letter and a word for longer than teachers think. There is a mystery hurdle in here which could only be unpicked in an elegant, developmental research study. The problem is not simple or obvious, and occurs despite a great deal of teacher talk about it. Some children who are reading and writing quite well still confuse the concepts of a letter and a word after 18 months at school. The reason may be simple but the explanation is elusive. Other print concepts, like punctuation, are mastered through more reading and writing experiences.

Studies of school entrants over more than 20 years show small increases in the average 'entry to school' scores in New Zealand, and increasing average scores on the C.A.P. after entry to school. Most children acquire the critical concepts before they have been at school for six months, mastering the advanced concepts gradually over the next 18 months. C.A.P. plays its important role early in reading acquisition. What is clear is that if you are not learning to attend to appropriate aspects of print this hampers the development of a sound literacy processing system. When it comes to reading and writing you are in a state of 'cognitive confusion' (Downing and Leong, 1982).

Two references of the past decade conclude this account. Johnston (1997) devotes a chapter of his book, *Knowing Literacy*, to concepts about print, and makes the important point that the conventions which are so obvious to adults are 'less than obvious' to young children. In one interaction between himself and one child, Dane, he analysed 19 things that he observed about how this child was attending to print. He discussed 'eddies and confusions' that can arise for children, including things as extreme as trying to read the white spaces, and believing that reading is memorising (as when a child places the closed book on the table and says, 'I can read this with the book shut'). He ends the discussion with three good questions:

1 Is the student actively theorising about the organisation of written language?
2 What confusions does the student have about the organisation of written language?
3 Is there anything in our talk about written language that might cause confusion?

Stallman and Pearson (1990) included C.A.P. as 'an outlier' in a review of formal measures of early literacy, even though it is not reviewed in Buros (the reference text of 'good' tests). They note several 'deviant features' of this 'alternative' test: it is not used in New Zealand as a readiness test but as a check on progress, it is administered in the context of 'reading' a real book, and it is an example of a situated assessment for individual students. Each five-year-old sits alongside the examiner and is asked to help by pointing to certain features as the book is read by the examiner. The authors write:

> We are convinced, based at least in part on our dissatisfaction with what is currently available, that the most productive methods of assessing early literacy lie in individual assessment of children while they are engaged in a literacy activity ... Only those [tests] in Marie Clay's battery come close to meeting such a standard ... we need more work in this area so that we can develop approaches that are even more situated than Clay's.

> (Stallman and Pearson, 1990, pages 41-42)

5   How might teachers of new entrants use this information?

The New Zealand Ministry of Education distributed a School Entry Assessment (SEA) survey to schools in 1997 and included in that survey the Concepts About Print task (C.A.P.). Many New Zealand teachers already use the C.A.P. as part of a survey of observations made after children have been at school for a year, and think of it as designed to help teachers observe the progress of young children in literacy learning.

There are benefits to be had from using C.A.P. within a month or two of a child arriving at school. C.A.P. should not be used to predict who will learn to read and write, and who might have difficulty because each child must learn to work within the conventions used in printed English. To have each child become a successful reader and writer *teachers must aim to make any such a prediction false.* They must teach so that all children become knowledgeable about these essential concepts and by doing so they open doors to literacy.

Teachers appear to have a good understanding of the importance of concepts about print among their students. Their activities introduce children early to how to approach their written texts in both reading and writing. Children expand this learning throughout their first year at school but have more advanced concepts to learn in the second year at school.

However, more concepts would be known by more children earlier if the lowest-achieving children could receive help and careful monitoring in that first six months of school. Giving more focused help to the least well-prepared more quickly in the first year of school will lead to greater earlier success for that group. Those who take a long time are likely to be children with many different characteristics. For example children who turn away from focused and sedentary activities, and those who have not yet discovered a liking for book-browsing, story reading and story telling, could be slower to form the early literacy concepts. And so would children who find it difficult to pull ideas together in a focused way, or children who miss too many days at school to make links between the things they do. Other children who could have difficulty might have been immersed in an oral culture in homes where written texts are rare, or those who are afraid to write or do not like to write. There are many reasons why children fail to give this learning their attention.

A teacher who knows where each child is starting from in this orientation to print area is better prepared to observe gradual change as it takes place.

Would this perhaps mean that the number of children who reach their sixth birthday and need to be referred to an early intervention programme like Reading Recovery would drop? Well, no. Contrary to some ill-informed opinion, the children who go into Reading Recovery have not yet failed anything. They have been learning but not fast enough to keep up with classmates who are racing ahead. So if teachers lift the speed at which these children orient to text and learn to find their way around it, and even lift their C.A.P. scores by the time they are six years of age, that would not necessarily reduce the number of children entering Reading Recovery.

First, orienting to texts is only one of the steps needed in constructing a reading and writing process – there are other important things to learn about letters, words, sounds and meanings, and how we put language things together. Teachers work on all these things too.

Secondly, and more important, what Reading Recovery represents is an insurance that the scores of the lowest 20 percent of children beginning in any school will not drag down the average performance overall. So if we lift the average literacy achievements in our schools to higher average levels we would still need to take out about a 20 percent insurance on our lowest achievers to support such a lift in general achievements. Critics of Reading Recovery miss that obvious point about the relativity of who gets into Reading Recovery.

For academic reasons many research studies search for components of literacy processing which predict success/failure in literacy learning, and this usually means what instrument correlates highly with progress. Such an instrument is used to sift out strong measures from weak measures, strong programmes from weak programmes, and strong learners from weak learners. To yield a high correlation the sample used in a research must range widely from very high scoring to very poor scoring among the individuals.

A prediction device is not useful when the teacher's task is to seek at all costs to spoil its prediction! That teacher needs a wide-spectrum battery of tasks that will direct her teaching, enabling her to use a learner's strengths in the service of that learner's weaknesses. With specific attention to conceptual, visual and motor learning inherent in print awareness, in addition to all the language-related skills, the teacher's task is not to predict who will fail but to bring every child to act upon information in print at high speed – *particularly the ones predicted by the prediction measure to be low performers.*

It is clear from studies of C.A.P. in different countries like New Zealand, the United Kingdom, the United States, Canada, Denmark and Israel that when the societal expectation is that children will not become readers and writers until a certain age, it is that expectation, and not age, that determines what is learned and how early it is learned.

Appendices

APPENDIX 1

– Administration Instructions – *Sand/Stones*   28

APPENDIX 2

– Concepts About Print Score Sheet – *Sand/Stones*   30

APPENDIX 3

– Quick Reference for Scoring Standards – *Sand/Stones*   31

Say to the child: '*I'm going to read you this story but I want you to help me.*'

COVER

Item 1   Test: For orientation of book. Pass the book to the child, holding it vertically by outside edge, spine towards the child.

       Say: '*Show me the front of this book.*'

       Score: 1 point for the correct response.

PAGES 2/3

Item 2   Test: Concept that print, not picture, carries the message.

       Say: '*I'll read this story. You help me. Show me where to start reading. Where do I begin to read?*'

Read the text on page 2.

       Score: 1 point for print. 0 for picture.

PAGES 4/5

Item 3   Test: For directional rules.

       Say: '*Show me where to start.*'

       Score: 1 point for top left.

Item 4   Test: Moves left to right on any line.

       Say: '*Which way do I go?*'

       Score: 1 point for left to right.

Item 5   Test: Return sweep.

       Say: '*Where do I go after that?*'

       Score: 1 point for return sweep to left, or for moving down the page.

(Score items 3-5 if all movements are demonstrated in one response.)

Item 6   Test: Word-by-word pointing.

       Say: '*Point to it while I read it.*'

Read the text on page 4 slowly but fluently.

       Score: 1 point for exact matching.

PAGE 6

Item 7   Test: Concept of first and last.

Read the text on page 6.

       Say: '*Show me the first part of the story.*' '*Show me the last part.*'

       Score: 1 point if BOTH are correct in any sense, that is, applied to the whole text or to a line, or to a word, or to a letter.

PAGE 7

Item 8   Test: Inversion of picture.

       Say: (slowly and deliberately) '*Show me the bottom of the picture.*' (DO NOT MENTION UPSIDE-DOWN.)

       Score: 1 point for verbal explanation, OR for pointing to top of page, OR for turning the book around and pointing appropriately.

PAGES 8/9

Item 9   Test: Response to inverted print.

       Say: '*Where do I begin?*' '*Which way do I go?*' '*Where do I go after that?*'

       Score: 1 point for beginning with 'The' (*Sand*), or 'I' (*Stones*), and moving right to left across the lower and then the upper line. OR 1 point for turning the book around and moving left to right in the conventional manner.

Read the text on page 8 now.

PAGES 10/11

Item 10   Test: Line sequence.

       Say: '*What's wrong with this?*'

Read immediately the bottom line first, then the top line. Do NOT point.

       Score: 1 point for comment on line order.

PAGES 12/13

Item 11   Test: A left page is read before a right page.

       Say: '*Where do I start reading?*'

       Score: 1 point for indicating the left page.

Item 12   Test: Word sequence.

       Say: '*What's wrong on this page?*' (Point to **page number 12**, NOT the text.)

Read the text on page 12 slowly as if it were correctly printed.

       Score: 1 point for comment on either error.

Item 13   Test: Letter order. (Changes to first or last letters.)

       Say: '*What's wrong on this page?*' (Point to **page number 13**, NOT the text.)

Read the text on page 13 slowly as if it were correctly printed.

       Score: 1 point for any ONE re-ordering of letters that is noticed and explained.

Item 14   Test: Re-ordering of letters within a word.

Say: *'What's wrong with the writing on this page?'*

Read the text on page 14 slowly as if it were correctly printed.

Score: 1 point for ONE error noticed.

Item 15   Test: Meaning of a question mark.

Say: *'What's this for?'* (Point to or trace the question mark with a finger or pencil.)

Score: 1 point for explanation of function or name.

Test: Punctuation.

Read the text on page 16.

Say: *'What's this for?'*

Item 16   Point to or trace with a pencil, the full stop (period).

Item 17   Point to or trace with a pencil, the comma.

Item 18   Point to or trace with a pencil, the quotation marks.

Item 19   Test: Capital and lower case letters.

Say: *'Find a little letter like this.'*
Sand: Point to capital T and demonstrate by pointing to an upper case T and a lower case t if the child does not succeed.
Stones: As above for S and s.

Say: *'Find a little letter like this.'*
Sand: Point to capital M, H in turn.
Stones: Point to capital T, B in turn.

Score: *Sand*:   1 point if BOTH m and h are located.
Stones: 1 point if BOTH t and b are located.

Item 20   Test: Words that contain the same letters in a different order.

Read the text on page 18.

Say: *'Show me* was.*'*
'Show me no.*'*

Score: 1 point for BOTH correct.

Have two pieces of light card (13 cm x 5 cm) that the child can hold and slide easily over the line of text to block out words and letters. To start, lay the cards on the page but leave all print exposed. Open the cards out between each question asked.

Item 21   Test: Letter concepts.

Say: *'This story says (Sand) "The waves splashed in the hole" [or (Stones) "The stone rolled down the hill"].* *'I want you to push the cards across the story like this until all you can see is* (deliberately with stress) *just one letter.'* (Demonstrate the movement of the cards but do not do the exercise.)

Say: *'Now show me two letters.'*

Score: 1 point if BOTH are correct.

Item 22   Test: Word concept.

Say: *'Show me just one word.'*
'Now show me two words.'

Score: 1 point if BOTH are correct.

Item 23   Test: First and last letter concepts.

Say: *'Show me the first letter of a word.'*
'Show me the last letter of a word.'

Score: 1 point if BOTH are correct.

Item 24   Test: Capital letter concepts.

Say: *'Show me a capital letter.'*

Score: 1 point if correct.

29

CONCEPTS ABOUT PRINT SCORE SHEET

Date: _____

Name: _____ Age: _____ TEST SCORE: ☐ /24

Recorder: _____ Date of Birth: _____ STANINE GROUP: ☐

PAGE	SCORE	ITEM	COMMENT
Cover		1. Front of book	
2/3		2. Print contains message	
4/5		3. Where to start	
4/5		4. Which way to go	
4/5		5. Return sweep to left	
4/5		6. Word-by-word matching	
6		7. First and last concept	
7		8. Bottom of picture	
8/9		9. Begins 'The' (*Sand*) or 'I' (*Stones*) bottom line, top OR turns book	
10/11		10. Line order altered	
12/13		11. Left page before right	
12/13		12. One change in word order	
12/13		13. One change in letter order	
14/15		14. One change in letter order	
14/15		15. Meaning of a question mark	
16/17		16. Meaning of full stop (period)	
16/17		17. Meaning of comma	
16/17		18. Meaning of quotation marks	
16/17		19. Locate m h (*Sand*) OR t b (*Stones*)	
18/19		20. Reversible words *was, no*	
20		21. One letter: two letters	
20		22. One word: two words	
20		23. First and last letter of word	
20		24. Capital letter	

QUICK REFERENCE FOR SCORING STANDARDS

Item	Pass standard
1	Front of book.
2	Print (not picture).
3	Points top left at 'I dug ...' (*Sand*) or 'I saw ...' (*Stones*).
4	Moves finger left to right on any line.
5	Moves finger from the right-hand end of a higher line to the left-hand end of the next lower line, or moves down the page.
6	Word-by-word matching.
7	Both concepts must be correct, but may be demonstrated on the whole text or on a line, word or letter.
8	Verbal explanation, or pointing to top of page, or turning the book around and pointing appropriately.
9	Score for beginning with 'The' (*Sand*) or 'I' (*Stones*) and moving right to left across the lower line and then the upper line, OR turning the book around and moving left to right in the conventional movement pattern.
10	Any explanation which implies that line order is altered.
11	Says or shows that a left page precedes a right page.
12	Notices at least one change of word order.
13	Notices at least one change in letter order.
14	Notices at least one change in letter order.
15	Says 'Question mark', or 'A question', or 'Asks something'.
16	Says 'Full stop', 'Period', 'It tells you when you've said enough' or 'It's the end'.
17	Says 'A little stop', or 'A rest', or 'A comma'.
18	Says 'That's someone talking', 'Talking', 'Speech marks'.
19	Locates two capital and lower case pairs.
20	Points correctly to **both** *was* and *no*.
21	Locates one letter and two letters on request.
22	Locates one word and two words on request.
23	Locates both a first and a last letter.
24	Locates one capital letter.

References

Clay, M.M. (1967). The reading behaviour of five-year-old children: A research report. *New Zealand Journal of Educational Studies*, 2, 11–31.

Clay, M.M. (1972). *The Early Detection of Reading Difficulties: A Diagnostic Survey.* Auckland: Heinemann.

Clay, M.M. (1972) *Sand*, (1979) *Stones*, (2000) *Follow Me, Moon*, (2000) *No Shoes*. Auckland: Heinemann.

Clay, M.M. (1974). Orientation to the spatial characteristics of the open book. *Visible Language*, 8, 275-282.

Clay, M.M. (1982). *Observing Young Readers - Selected Papers*. Portsmouth NH: Heinemann.

Clay, M.M. (1985). Engaging with the school system; A study of interactions in new entrant classrooms. *New Zealand Journal of Educational Studies*, 20, 1, 20-30.

Clay, M.M. (1989). Concepts About Print in English and Other Languages. *The Reading Teacher*, January, 268-276.

Clay, M.M. (1991). *Becoming Literate: The Construction of Inner Control*. Auckland: Heinemann.

Clay, M.M. (1993). *An Observation Survey of Early Literacy Achievement*. Auckland: Heinemann.

Clay, M.M. (1997). Using the Concepts About Print task with school entrants. *'Set Special': Language and Literacy*. Wellington: New Zealand Council for Educational Research.

Downing, J. and Leong, C.K. (1982). *Psychology of Reading*. New York: Macmillan.

Harris, T.L. and Hodges, R.E. (1995). (Eds). *The Literacy Dictionary: The Vocabulary of Reading and Writing*. Newark, Delaware: International Reading Association.

Johns, J.L. (1980). First graders' concepts about print. *Reading Research Quarterly*, 15, 4, 529-549.

Johnston, P.H. (1997). *Knowing Literacy; Constructive Literacy Assessment*. York, Maine: Stenhouse Publishers.

Koefoed, B. and Watson, B. (1999). *An Observation Survey: The Video*. Auckland: Heinemann.

Learning Media (1996). *The Learner as a Reader: Developing Reading Programmes*. Wellington: Learning Media.

Learning Media (1997). *School Entry Assessment Guide for Teachers (SEA)*. Wellington: Ministry of Education.

McNaughton, S. (1995). *Patterns of Emergent Literacy: Processes of Development and Transition*. Auckland: Oxford University Press.

Robinson, H.M. (1967). Insights from research: Children's behaviour while reading. In W.D. Page (Ed.), *Help for the Reading Teacher: New Directions in Research*. National Conference on Research in English.

Stallman, A.C. and Pearson, D.P. (1990). Formal measures of early literacy. In Morrow, L.M. and Smith, J.K. (1990) (Eds), *Assessment for Instruction in Early Literacy*. Englewood Cliffs, NJ: Prentice-Hall.

Watson, B. (1980). Teaching beginning reading: An observation study. MA thesis, University of Auckland Library.